Chakras

The Comprehensive Handbook Offering
Remarkable Strategies To Radiate Vitality, Amplify
The Aura, And Attune The Chakras

*(Elevate Positive Vibrations By Means Of Kundalini
Activation And The Practice Of Reiki Meditation)*

Vittorino Sandri

TABLE OF CONTENT

Chakra Healing 3

2: Chakra Stones 22

Steps to Open Chakras..................................... 60

Balancing The Chakras................................... 91

Healing the Third Chakra........................... 140

What does the concept of spiritual consciousness entail?.................................. 166

CHAKRA HEALING

The practice of chakra healing has been employed for an extensive duration to harmonize crucial energetic centers within our body known as chakras. We have at our disposal an array of different tools, such as stones or the practice of meditation in conjunction with chakra balancing. The end result will be an improvement in physical well-being and a heightened sense of inner peace and contentment.

According to experts in chakra healing, it is believed that each individual possesses seven fundamental chakras which align with significant areas of their physical bodies, as well as their emotional and spiritual aspects. The seven chakras encompass a vertical axis that spans from the sacrum to the cranial apex. Chakras possess their distinct shades, vibrational frequency, and emblem. An example of this is the primary chakra, which is located at the lower end of the spinal column and referred to as the foundational chakra. This particular chakra governs the functions and wellbeing of the spinal region, kidneys, lower extremities, rectum, and the immune system. Thus, when there is an imbalance in this particular chakra, it can precipitate symptoms such as lower back pain, the development of varicose veins, instances of leg cramps, rectal ailments, manifestations of depression, as well as disorders relating to the immune system. The lack of equilibrium in the root chakra can arise from feelings of diminished self-assurance, indecision, or familial preoccupations.

Various chakras encompass the sacral, solar plexus, cardiac, laryngeal, frontal, and coronal chakras. In order for the entire body to synchronize in harmony, it is imperative that each energy center resonates at its optimal frequency independently of one another. Thus, every chakra holds equal significance for the optimal functioning of the body, as stipulated by the principles of chakra healing.

There are a wide range of effective tools that have the potential to impact the vibration of the chakra, and this is where chakra balancing assumes paramount importance. Chakra stones, the human voice, music, melodies, mantras, and chakra meditation facilitate the reestablishment of the chakras into their respective harmonious vibrational alignment. An illustrative example is the significant impact of gemstones such as hematite, onyx, ruby, or garnet on the root chakra. During the process of chakra healing, a trained practitioner may employ any of these chakra stones to cleanse and harmonize your root chakra.

Chakra meditation can also serve as a technique to awaken and enhance the energetic portals within your chakra system, facilitating the harmonious circulation of beneficial metaphysical energy throughout your being. During the process of introspection, your attention is predominantly directed towards each individual chakra, commencing with the first and progressing systematically to the crown chakra. Through the visualization of the flow of energy from one chakra to another, individuals can effectively eliminate any obstructions present in each energy center that may give rise to both physical and emotional distress.

Given that the chakras govern the functioning of every organ and system within the body, chakra healing carries extensive health implications. Chakra harmonization can potentially contribute to the enhancement of cardiovascular, respiratory, cognitive, immune, and gastrointestinal function. Additionally, it may offer potential alleviation for conditions such as depression, anxiety, and other disturbances in emotional equilibrium. Numerous individuals hold the belief that the manipulation of chakras can have a profound and transformative impact on both one's physical well-being and overall spiritual state. When our chakras are in a state of harmonious alignment, we are able to attain elevated levels of awareness.

If the notion of harnessing the profound power of chakra healing resonates with you, we recommend seeking the services of a highly skilled practitioner in this realm. A proficient practitioner of healing will gather relevant information regarding your physical well-being in order to identify the chakras that are experiencing the most pronounced blockages or imbalances. Subsequently, an individual could employ a variety of techniques to facilitate harmonious resonance within your energy centers.

Two - Exploring the Seven Chakras

The principal energy centers of the human body consist of the seven chakras. Each of them possesses a particular geographic placement and embodies distinct and exceptional characteristics. When the chakras are completely activated, they have the capacity to foster heightened consciousness and induce tangible transformations within the body. When such an event takes place, our physical well-being reaches its peak, and our cognitive faculty attains a state of assured perception. The sensation of bodily discomfort becomes apparent to us when an obstruction is present, manifesting itself as a physical ailment. Hence, it is crucial to acquire knowledge and comprehension regarding the symbolic significance of each of these seven chakras, as well as the measures we can take to ensure the uninterrupted circulation of energy.

Fundamental Chakra – To Possess

The initial chakra, also known as the root chakra, derived its name from the Sanskrit term "Muladhara", signifying the fundamental or bedrock aspect. It represents the energy center associated with aspects of stability, protection, self-preservation, trust, determination to thrive, and a grounded sense of being. The sacral chakra can be found at the anatomical region known as the sacrum, positioned at the lowermost part of the vertebral column. Symbolically, it is depicted as a energetic sphere extending downwards, encompassing the lower limbs and the feet.

This particular chakra bears the responsibility of establishing the fundamental basis upon which our existence is constructed. It serves as the embodiment of our corporeal identity. When the root chakra is unblocked, we experience a sense of courage and security in delving into every facet of existence. This is the place where we cultivate self-preservation and anchor ourselves firmly to the earth.

The typical emblem associated with it is frequently depicted as a crimson-colored lotus flower bearing four petals. Red elicits an innate response and invigorates our vital force. It represents our life's pursuits and resilience.

In order to achieve equilibrium in the root chakra, it is essential to confront and expose our fears. Embark on a journey into the unknown, embracing and acknowledging all facets of your being that you have yet to fully embrace. Subsequently, extend benevolent and empathetic regards as you set them free into the realm of existence.

The Sacral Chakra and Holistic Approaches to Healing.

Color: Red

Element: Earth

Location: Situated at the base of the spinal column, in close proximity to the coccyx.

Emotional Afflictions caused by Hindrances: Apprehension, Insufficiency in Autonomy, Unease, Melancholy.

Physical Disorders Caused by Obstructions: Excessive weight, eating disorder characterized by self-imposed food restriction, gastrointestinal irregularity, nerve pain radiating down the leg, swollen and twisted veins, swollen blood vessels in the rectum, blood deficiency, hypersensitivity responses, ailments triggered by excessive stress.

Healing through the utilization of crystals: Garnet, Ruby, Hematite, Tiger's eye, starry obsidian, smoky quartz, obsidian rainbow, heliotrope, fire agate, black tourmaline.

Therapeutic Use of Herbal Remedies: Valerian and Elder Blossom

Exploring the Therapeutic Benefits of Bach Flower Remedy: Incorporating Rock Rose and Sweet Chestnut

The Therapeutic Benefits of Essential Oils: cypress, rosemary, cedarwood, and clove

Healing through Sonic Vibration: Recite the primordial seed sound - "LAM"

Healing Through the Power of Positive Declarations: "I have faith in the progression of life." "I experience a profound sense of safety, stability, and comfort within my physical being."

Stimulating the Root Chakra: Engage in a daily practice of foot massage for self-care. Make an effort to allocate a significant amount of your time engaging with the natural world. Establish direct connection with the ground through the act of walking without footwear, immersing your feet in a flowing body of water, or alternatively, by leaning against the trunk of a tree. Observe the Sunrise or Sunset. Immerse yourself in the enigmatic hue of crimson. Wearing the color red will prove advantageous for you as well.

Meditation/Yoga Asana: Apanasana (Knees to chest Pose)/Utkatasana (Chair Pose)

The Heart Chakra

As inferred from its nomenclature, the fourth chakra is situated within the cardiac region, symbolizing attributes encompassing love, benevolence, and compassion towards both individuals and creatures. In accordance with Hindu ideology, it is believed that the seat of the soul lies within the heart. This fourth chakra corresponds to the physiological aspects of your heart, lungs, arms, and glands. The Heart Chakra also symbolizes the intersection or convergence of our corporeal and metaphysical essence. Therefore, the fourth chakra serves as a conduit that connects the physical, mental, spiritual, and emotional aspects of an individual. The fourth chakra, commonly referred to as the heart chakra, establishes a vital link between the higher, spiritual chakras and the lower, physical chakras. Hence, the heart chakra constitutes an essential element of our physiological system, and its equilibrium plays a significant role in promoting the stability of the remaining chakras.

Situated within the central region, the fourth chakra facilitates the harmonization of benevolence and empathy towards others. You would experience a profound sense of inner tranquility which would extend harmoniously to your perception of the external world. In addition, it facilitates the attainment of success, advancement, progress, and equilibrium, thereby enabling us to assist others also. Consequently, the activation and equilibrium of your fourth chakra lead to the manifestation of humanitarian qualities within you. Nevertheless, an imbalance in this particular chakra can be attributed to an absence of harmony in either the initial three chakras individually or collectively in their entirety. Any disturbances within this chakra can lead to emotional instability, a sense of being unloved, or a tendency to harbor suspicion and regression towards various aspects of life.

Nevertheless, in the event that your fourth chakra exhibits excessive activity, there is a likelihood that your affection may be causing feelings of confinement in others, potentially indicating that your love emanates from a place of self-interest. Therefore, achieving equilibrium in the fourth chakra pertaining to the Heart is an essential element for both your spiritual and physical welfare. Should there be an imbalance in your fourth chakra, it is plausible that you may encounter complications pertaining to your pulmonary, cardiac, or immunological functions.

The Throat Chakra

The throat chakra, which is the fifth energy center within our body, is closely connected with the faculties of self-expression and communication. Moreover, it also connotes artistic expression, sound judgement, self-assurance, integrity, and sagacity. Thus, in the event that the fifth chakra is activated and operating optimally, individuals may be characterized by their ease in communicating and their ability to maintain harmonious interpersonal relationships. Conversely, in the event of an underactive throat chakra, one tends to exhibit reticence and lacks confidence in engaging in verbal communication. An additional intriguing aspect to acknowledge regarding this chakra is that excessive lack of veracity in one's speech may potentially result in its under-activation.

The scenario involving an excessively active throat chakra pertains to individuals who engage in excessive verbal communication, potentially as a means to create interpersonal distance. Individuals of this nature tend to demonstrate a deficiency in attentive listening skills, persistently engaging in dialogue without earnestly considering the perspectives of others. Whilst possessing a well-functioning throat chakra is advantageous, a deficient throat chakra can give rise to various health complications including recurring colds, throat inflammation or infection, impediments in speech, imbalances in the thyroid gland, perpetual fatigue, and an enduring sense of despondency. Insufficient circulation of energy manifests as a profound sense of apprehension and unease within an individual, leading to the adoption of introverted tendencies characterized by reticence in communication and aversion to change.

The obstruction of the throat chakra can also manifest in individuals through deceitfulness, hindered creativity, and difficulties in effectively expressing their needs to others. Consequently, the most effective method to restore equilibrium to the fifth chakra and ensure its optimal wellness involves engaging in activities such as singing, engaging with calming melodies, contemplating the sky during the dawn and dusk, and diligently attending to one's breath. Meditation serves as an additional potent remedy for the fifth chakra and is highly recommended for individuals experiencing an under-functioning fifth chakra.

2: CHAKRA STONES

Chakra stones encompass a wide array of stones exhibiting a multitude of colors, serving as instrumental aids in the practice of chakra healing.

The human physique is equipped with chakras, each of which is associated with distinct hues. In instances where these chakras are not functioning in accordance with their designated purposes, there will be a noticeable alteration in their respective hues.

Chakra stones are designed to aid in the restoration of equilibrium within your chakras, thereby promoting an enhanced state of serenity and concordance. Chakra misalignment can occur due to their commonly described nature as rotating centers of energy. Additionally, they have the potential to experience a decline in performance as they transition into a lethargic turn or rapidly rotate.

The disruption in equilibrium of a chakra is commonly experienced as each of these energy centers aligns with distinct facets of our being, encompassing the spiritual, emotional, physical, and mental aspects.

The utilization of chakra stones will prove advantageous in equipping you to anticipate and effectively address such circumstances as you acquire further knowledge on their practical applications. Each chakra, as previously instructed, possesses its individual color symbolism. Additionally, every chakra possesses distinct symptoms of dysfunction, necessitating careful observation on your part to identify any recurring problems or illnesses. Once you have acquired precise knowledge regarding the affected chakra, it is imperative to carefully select the specific gemstone that possesses the ability to alleviate, purify, and restore equilibrium to said chakra.

Chakra stones may be selected from a diverse range of crystalline specimens in varying quantities, as the primary objective rests upon achieving optimal equilibrium to effectively support the functioning of one's chakras. In the event that you happen to possess and preserve gemstones with the intention of their aesthetic value rather than their therapeutic properties, it may come as a surprise to discover that certain specimens possess attributes capable of addressing imbalances within one or more of your chakras.

Regardless of their price, rarity, or aesthetic appeal, all chakra stones possess the same intrinsic value and serve an equal purpose. If you possess the appropriate hue, you possess the capability to harmonize your chakra as necessitated.

Root Chakra Stone

The appropriate chakra stones that will facilitate the alignment of your root chakra are those of a red and black hue. You will experience an enhanced sense of groundedness, solidity, stability, and self-esteem.

The chakra stones recommended for the root chakra encompass Ruby, Black Obsidian, Hematite, Smoky Quartz, Red Jasper, Jet, Black Onyx, Fire Opal, Bloodstone, and Red Garnet.

It is necessary for you to position any of the aforementioned stones for your root chakra in close proximity to your groin and between your thighs. Consider the hues of crimson or ebony as you contemplate your profound essence, an intensified ardency towards all matters, a state of increased felicity and fortitude beneath.

Chakra stone specifically designed for the stimulation and balance of the sacral chakra

When the Sacral Chakra exhibits excessive activity, one will frequently experience feelings of frustration, while insufficient activity in the second chakra may give rise to a sense of joylessness.

There exist diverse types of chakra stones that are effective in facilitating the alignment of your sacral chakra. These stones encompass Orange Calcite, Orange Aventurine, Tiger's Eye, Orange Jasper, Carnelian, Sunstone, Fire Opal, Tangerine Quartz, and Brown Citrine.

Upon achieving alignment of your Sacral Chakra, you will experience a surge of inspiration, enhanced motivation, and the requisite level of excitement.

Solar Plexus Chakra Crystal

When one's Solar Plexus Chakra is properly aligned, they will experience the emergence of innovative and outstanding ideas. The appropriate Chakra Stones to employ for the purpose of healing your Solar Plexus are the yellow gemstones, such as Yellow Jasper, Amber, Golden Calcite, Rutilated Quartz, Moonstone, Citrine, Fire Opal, Pyrite, and Topaz.

Attaining alignment of your Solar Plexus Chakra will empower you to experience a sense of purpose, motivation, and self-assurance. To utilize these stones for your Solar Plexus Chakra, assume a supine position and position the stone at a distance of 2 inches from the location of your abdominal region. Envision the hue of yellow within your thoughts, accompanied by a highly luminous and radiant sun.

Heart Chakra Chakra Stones

When one's chakra is in a state of harmonious alignment, an individual becomes predisposed to being receptive, tranquil, and prepared to embrace new interpersonal connections, nurture wholesome relationships, readily extend forgiveness, and experience profound love.

In order to facilitate the alignment of your heart chakra, we suggest utilizing the following Chakra stones that have been recommended: Green Aventurine, Emerald, Peridot, Rhodonite, Green Tourmaline, Rose Quartz, Green Moss Agate, Pink Tourmaline, Jade, Ruby, Chrysoprase, Malachite,

Rhodochrosite, and Watermelon Tourmaline.

You will experience emotional rejuvenation, enhance your interpersonal connections, and exude affection.

Crystals for Balancing the Throat Chakra

In the event of an unstable Throat Chakra, you may encounter challenges in effectively articulating your thoughts, which can result in the occurrence of miscommunication and feelings of frustration.

Opting for blue chakra stones can facilitate the stabilization of your Throat Chakra. The aforementioned gemstones comprise Blue Aragonite, Lapis Lazuli, Angelite,

Blue Apatite, Blue Calcite, Turquoise, Aquamarine, Sodalite, Blue Sapphire, and Blue Lace Agate.

When your throat chakra is in a state of alignment, the process of communication and self-expression becomes effortless.

Emma's Instability

Our initial target audience consists of individuals such as Emma, who is 28 years old and holds a secure position in a prominent marketing firm within a corporate environment. Emma is currently unmarried, and it has been six years since she departed from the university. She resides on her own in a luxurious seaside apartment, the furnishings of which have been generously provided by her parents. From an external perspective, it may appear that Emma has all aspects of her life in order. She maintains a respectable occupation, resides autonomously in a favorable district, and appears to relish the rewards of her efforts alongside a genuine, tight-knit social circle. Emma, nonetheless, harbors a profound sense of discontentment with her existence, propelled by emotions of culpability, envy, and an enduring perception of her inadequacy. The notion that Emma's inability to achieve a promotion within her marketing firm appears to be a contributing factor to these sentiments, given her tenure of more than five years with the company.

Emma grapples with an enduring apprehension of a lifetime of solitude, which has led her to relocate residences seven times in dwellings characterized by challenges that, in hindsight, she believes she might have overcome more effectively had she possessed better emotional fortitude. It appears that Emma's acquaintances are predominantly preoccupied with their personal endeavors and not inclined to be encumbered by her concerns. It seems as though they are primarily focused on advancing their careers, indulging in luxury vehicles, fashionable attire, and extravagant dining experiences, as well as striving to make a lasting impression on their professional peers. Emma perceives them as exhibiting unbridled avarice, an excessive preoccupation with material possessions, and an insatiable thirst for power, to an extent that their grip on reality seems to have waned. Emma's romantic endeavors have been sporadic at most, as gentlemen swiftly lose interest whenever she reveals her vulnerabilities and attempts to discuss her feelings of unease or apprehension. This, undoubtedly, casts a negative light on the individuals whom she has elected to associate with. Nevertheless, there are multiple actions that Emma ought to have undertaken personally in order to ascertain the underlying source of her anxiety and apprehension. Emma, buoyed by both the anticipation of the approaching summer climate and the subsequent surge in her optimistic sentiment, resolves to assert control over her circumstances. She is not seeking any medication, as she holds the belief that it is preferable to facilitate natural healing processes.

Emma elects to go for a stroll around her residential area on a particularly sunlit weekend. She foregoes any music or exercise equipment; instead, she rises from her customary place on the bed and departs from the residence. Lacking any specific itinerary or predetermined path, Emma inadvertently stumbles upon previously uncharted areas within the locality. The woman unexpectedly encounters an exquisite display of potted plants and consequently makes the impromptu decision to commence her own vegetable garden upon the balcony of her residence. Upon Emma's return to her abode, she experiences a profound sensation of tranquility, solace, and buoyancy during her contemplation of the stroll she embarked upon. Additionally, she has made a commitment to partake in a leisurely stroll every Saturday morning.

In the ensuing weeks, Emma secures a promotion at her workplace, places a down payment to procure her existing apartment, and enrolls in a fitness center. She has at last attained a sense of belonging, obtained steadfastness in her employment, and successfully dispelled any lingering sentiments of guilt, apprehension, and unease. Emma has taken the initiative to ground herself, facilitating the opening of her root chakra. She is currently engaged in a deliberate effort to achieve equilibrium through various activities, including leisurely walks, regular exercises, and conscientious fulfillment of responsibilities.

Emma has effectively discovered the means to unlock her root chakra. Through such actions, she unveiled numerous opportunities in her life that she believed were unattainable. The process commences by acknowledging and accepting the factors that have impeded her progress. Apprehensions, uncertainties, and distress often provide the explanation.

The subsequent inquiry pertains to the origins of these fears and anxieties. Could it be attributed to our early developmental experiences? Is it due to our deviation from the societal norms or expectations? Could it be attributed to our perception of ourselves? By engaging in unbiased introspection, we can ascertain resolutions to these inquiries. If one lacks proficiency in self-reflection, the assistance of a mediator, a confidant, or a therapist can aid in this endeavor. Subsequently, we can divert our attention towards the task of activating our chakras.

Aromatherapy for the Harmonization of Chakras

Aromatherapy employs fragrant essences derived from botanical sources with the purpose of harmonizing, elevating, and restoring the energy centers of the body, thereby fostering a sense of happiness, tranquility, and vitality. As evidenced by the impact of colors on chakra points/energy centers, various aromatherapy essences elicit a comparably profound influence on these focal areas. Individuals exhibit diverse responses to different substances.

Each category of essential oil generates distinct energy patterns that vibrate at subtly varying frequencies. The oscillations generate energy patterns that correspond to the energy patterns of your seven primary chakras. The pristine harmonics of essential oils can serve to realign the frequencies of your chakras/energy patterns.

Presented herewith are several crucial essential oils along with the corresponding chakras they evoke.

Root chakra: Essential oils such as frankincense, sage, cardamom, clove, ginger, patchouli, rosewood, and carrot can be used for the stimulation and balancing of the root chakra.

Sacral chakra: Some examples of essential oils associated with this chakra include Melissa, jasmine, tangerine, rose, geranium, cinnamon, and vanilla, among others.

The navel chakra is associated with scents such as sandalwood, lavender, rosemary, oregano, peppermint, cinnamon, thyme, black pepper, juniper, myrrh, and numerous others.

Heart chakra: Essential oils such as ylang ylang, vanilla, sandalwood, rose, neroli, melissa, lavender, jasmine, geranium, chamomile, and bergamot have been found to be beneficial in balancing and harmonizing the energy associated with the heart chakra.

Throat chakra: Essential oils such as German and Roman Chamomile, cypress, lavender, frankincense, mandarin, tea tree, sandalwood, spruce, geranium, among others.

Brow (Third Eye) Chakra: The essential oils that can be used to balance and harmonize the Brow Chakra are frankincense, sage, spruce, rose, rosemary, clary, oregano, thyme, pine, lavender, marjoram, and cedar.

Crown Chakra: The recommended essential oils for balancing and aligning the crown chakra are myrrh, spruce, lavender, ravensara, rosemary, frankincense, jasmine, sandalwood, rose, and basil.

Presented herein is a method utilizing aromatherapy that can be employed to promote the healing, augmentation, and harmonization of your chakra centers.

1. Select the necessary essential oils that you intend to utilize. It is advisable to select a singular variety of oil for each chakra during each session.

2. Craft your own sacred blend of anointing oil. Combine each essential oil with a carrier oil such

as grape seed or jojoba oil, ensuring a dilution ratio of 1 - 10 drops of essential oil per ounce of the carrier oil. Please ensure that every blend is appropriately labeled.

3. Place the fused anointing oil in a conveniently accessible location subsequent to assuming a reclined position.

4. It is advised to don loose-fitting attire for optimal comfort, while also being mindful of the possibility of oil stains or damage. Subsequently, recline upon a surface that provides utmost comfort to you. One can enhance comfort by placing a pillow and a blanket underneath their head and knees. Please allocate a few moments to engage in slow and deep breathing exercises, focusing

on inhaling and exhaling from your abdominal area, causing it to visibly expand and contract.

5. Establish the objective for the therapeutic session. If your intention is solely to focus on one chakra, it is imperative that you establish a clear and specific objective dedicated exclusively to that particular energy center. If your intention is to address the entirety of the system, then establish an overarching objective for this process of restoration.

6. Administer the chakra essential oil to the designated all energy centers. Please administer a limited amount of the substance gradually, using your fingertips, in a clockwise motion specifically to the indicated area.

7. For the root chakra, you may apply the oil by gently massaging it either on the lower back or onto the soles of your feet.

8. If one intends to focus on the complete system of chakras, one may opt to commence the sequence either with the crown chakra descending to the root chakra in sequential arrangement, or inversely, from the root chakra ascending to the crown chakra. It is contingent upon your perception of what is morally correct.

9. As you consecrate each chakra point within your physical being, it may be necessary to articulate your intentions for its healing, and perceive the energy emanating from the oil assimilating into your being. Envision the synchronized

flow of the applied essential oil, harmonizing and aligning your chakras to achieve equilibrium, expansion, and attunement.

10. Once all the points in your body have been meticulously anointed with the essential oil, it is advisable to proceed by granting yourself a period of repose, wherein the oils can effectively expunge any disturbances within your energy field and restore equilibrium. Maintain a consistent and measured breathing pattern while making a deliberate effort to clear your mind as extensively as you can.

11. Once you perceive that you have successfully achieved your predetermined objective, conclude the session.

12. Redirect your attention and consciousness to the present moment, facilitating a gradual transition back into your routine existence. Following the session, you have the option to partake in consuming a piece of fruit or alternatively, avail yourself of a glass of water.

13. It may be necessary to document your session experiences within your personal journal.

14. Observe over a span of approximately two weeks as positive transformations begin to manifest.

Recieve and Release:

Receive with Your Palms:

A palm can be likened to an expansive vessel that receives the boundless energy of the cosmos, beckons for supplication, and serves as a receptacle for all that befalls upon oneself. Inquire with open hands, now that you are aware that miracles already reside within your grasp and now that you can comprehend the reasoning behind individuals such as those with spiritual beliefs, including practitioners of Christianity, Islam, and others, using its power, whether inadvertently or deliberately.

Release with Your Feet:

Ensure that your feet remain unobstructed in order to enhance your physical well-being, attain higher levels of success, accomplish your objectives, and draw favorable circumstances into your sphere of existence. Regardless of the methodology that resonates with you, whether it involves grounding oneself through walking barefoot and communing with nature, or humbly acknowledging the vastness of the universe and seeking its assistance in removing obstacles.

Every chakras job:

Now, it is evident to you that your palms and the soles of your feet are intricately connected with all seven chakras within your body, rendering them highly significant. "Now let us commence in a systematic manner, beginning from the uppermost position and progressing downwards:

Crown Chakra:

Situated: At the crown of the cranium

Some refer to it as the "Divine nexus", where spiritual energy permeates one's being, fostering a profound connection with one's divine creator, higher consciousness, and the celestial wisdom. As such, the energy infiltrates your physical form through two distinct regions: OR Consequently, the energy permeates your body originating from two specific areas:

Palm of Your Hands

Crown Chakra

Now that we have clarified this matter, let us proceed to discussing the indicators of low energy in your crown chakra.

Indications of an imbalanced crown chakra:

- Headache

- Unable to focus

- The incapacity to perceive the veracity and possess a discerning perspective

Experiencing resentment towards God and distancing oneself from a spiritual connection.

Balancing Method:

- Engage in meditation or engage in prayer if you adhere to a specific religious belief

- Express appreciation towards a higher power, the cosmos, the divine, the Supreme Being.

- It is widely believed that assuming a headstand position may provide assistance, although it cannot achieve perfect equilibrium. It is advisable to exercise caution and refrain from placing full reliance on the system, as it may only provide a modest 10% measure of balance.

Balanced Crown Chakra Indicators:

- Experiencing a sense of interconnectedness with the divine and the cosmic realm.

- Witnessing the majesty of deity and the manifestation of divine abilities in your daily existence.

- Lightness

Third Eye

Located: on the forehead

Upon receiving the energy from your crown chakra, it proceeds to your third eye chakra. The activation of the third eye chakra is a rarity among individuals, as it poses significant challenges. It is noteworthy that those who possess this activation typically did so during their early adolescence. It represents the ability to comprehend events without direct observation. It is evident that there is a lack of transparency in people's motives and future events. It is referred to by some as the sixth sense.

Indications of an imbalanced third eye chakra:

- Lacking the knowledge and understanding required to make a decision.

- Incapable of determining your subsequent course of action.

- Regrettably, one is currently unable to obtain an accurate understanding of the present situation as well as anticipate forthcoming events.

Balancing Method:

- Meditation

- Engaging in supplication and beseeching a higher power or universal force for guidance and understanding.

Indicators of a well-balanced third eye chakra:

- Listening to and having faith in the inner voice within oneself.

- Gaining clarity regarding your desires - Achieving a clear sense of what you seek - Ensuring a clear understanding of your aspirations - Attaining a clear vision of your objectives

- Witnessing the most profound essence of existence - Observing the pinnacle portrayal of life - Beholding the epitome of life's composition

- Possessing a sharp sense of intuition

Throat Chakra:

Situated at the midpoint of the neck.

Upon the transmission of energy from the crown chakra to the third eye, it subsequently descends to the heart chakra. Allow me to elucidate and present the information in a concise manner, facilitating your comprehension of its significance and underlying concept. Do you possess a reserved disposition? Do you encounter difficulty in articulating your emotions? If such is the case, I urge you to read this attentively as it undoubtedly pertains to you. The inability to effectively articulate oneself and the lack of fluency in speech are indicative of the messages your throat chakra is attempting to convey. Individuals who frequently experience subjugation or exploitation within their professional or domestic settings, or any other circumstances, often manifest throat chakra-related issues. However, what is the nexus between these issues and the throat itself? The throat chakra is influenced by various factors, with freedom being a pivotal aspect. When one's freedom is restricted, either emotionally or physically, it can manifest through symptoms that serve as indicators of this limitation.

Indications of an imbalanced throat chakra:

- Experiencing limitations on one's ability to engage in unrestricted conversation.

- Challenges in articulating one's thoughts and emotions

- Experiencing a sense of confinement in being unable to

express your deeply-felt, yet unspoken, thoughts.

Balancing Method:

- Please engage in enthusiastic singing and give it your utmost effort!

- Express your emotions audibly and release them in their entirety.

- Feel free to express your thoughts openly and without reservation.

STEPS TO OPEN CHAKRAS

Prior to delving into a detailed analysis of each of the 7 chakras, it is imperative to comprehend that exerting excessive effort or placing undue strain in the endeavor to activate one's chakras can potentially yield a contrary outcome. The objective of adhering to the chakra system is to establish and sustain an equilibrium that guarantees comprehensive welfare of the psyche and physique, wherein this equilibrium may entail the asymmetrical contribution of the diverse chakras.

In a comparable manner, it is advisable to refrain from altering chakras that are excessively active, as they likely serve as compensation for chakras that are closed or only partially active. The objective is to establish equilibrium among the chakras and ensure their optimal functioning as a cohesive system.

5: An Exploration of the Root Chakra (Red)

The root chakra is symbolized by the color red and governs our sense of ease and security in diverse circumstances. It facilitates heightened bodily awareness and facilitates the acquisition of greater levels of control. By opening this chakra, you will achieve a state of enhanced stability, security, and discernment in your actions.

You experience a positive sentiment towards the individuals in your surroundings, resulting in an enhanced ability to place trust in them. You experience a heightened sense of environmental awareness and become cognizant of the occurrences in your vicinity. To summarize, the activation of the root chakra will facilitate the establishment of a profound bond between yourself and your physical being.

In the event that it is rendered inactive or merely partially ajar, what would be the course of action? In the event that the root chakra remains inactive, one is prone to experiencing detrimental patterns of thought. "You are likely to experience increased anxiety and frequently find yourself in a state of apprehension." Additionally, it is probable that you will emanate a discouraging countenance and exhibit resistance towards individuals.

In brief, a deficiency in proper control of this chakra may lead to the manifestation of an insecure demeanor that avoids social interactions and obstructs the cultivation of relationships on a daily basis, subsequently impeding one's progress in social, emotional, and individual growth.

Generally, excessively active chakras are not typically regarded as ideal. In the present scenario, should you possess an excessively stimulated root chakra, it will manifest in qualities of avarice and a focus on material gains. You will exhibit an overwhelming sense of ambition and an insatiable thirst for power. Notably, such dispositions also give rise to solitude, as individuals are unable to establish meaningful connections with you. This shift towards materialism subsequently results in a withdrawal from social interactions due to apprehensions about the enmity and envy of others. The resultant lack of depth diminishes our ability to appreciate human connections and instills a lasting sense of emptiness.

An excessively stimulated root chakra is also prone to engendering a heightened resistance towards change, as it fosters a deceptive perception of control over one's life and manifests as excessive self-assurance, particularly in matters concerning the individual. Regrettably, as the individual becomes consumed by materialism, their ability to transcend material desires and gain mastery over their impulses becomes significantly arduous.

To initiate the activation of the red chakra, it is crucial for one to gain control and mastery over their physical being. For individuals seeking to cultivate their root chakra, the paramount practice entails establishing a profound connection with one's physical being. Engage in physical exercises and activities such as yoga, brisk walking, or consistently maintaining cleanliness in your living environment.

Engaging in these physical activities will facilitate the establishment of a connection between oneself and their own physical entity, increasing the likelihood of activating the root chakra. Yogis uphold the belief in diligently practicing a comprehensive range of exercises on a daily basis, thereby ensuring the optimal opening of the root chakra.

Additionally, there are a number of established and validated exercises that can effectively enhance the activation of the red chakra. This particular technique is commonly referred to as "grounding oneself." The objective of this method is to establish a sense of alignment between your physical form and the surface upon which you stand. We engage in this action frequently throughout the day; however, it is crucial to intimately perceive the underlying circumstances and strive to establish a meaningful bond.

This practice is predominantly employed by schools of thought aligned with Buddhism, as its efficacy relies on the cultivation of mindfulness through the engagement with mundane activities. The Buddhist tradition has nurtured and imparts the practice of mindfulness, an independent form of meditation that concurrently serves as a means to cultivate a heightened connection between the mind and the body in daily existence.

To execute this exercise, assume an upright posture (if feasible, without footwear) and allow yourself to unwind. Now, assume a slight crouching position while shifting your pelvis forward. By assuming this stance, you are effectively distributing your body weight equitably across both of your feet. Now proceed ahead slightly and maintain this stance for a minimum duration of 3 to 4 minutes.

The subsequent action following this would entail assuming a seated position on the ground, with the legs crossed in the customary stance associated with Yoga practices. Place the apex of your index finger in contact with the apex of your thumb, ensuring that both hands are comfortably placed upon your knees. This is the opportune period to direct your concentration towards the focal point of the root chakra, specifically the region encompassing your pelvic area.

As you gradually regain composure, it is now appropriate to gently utter the sound 'LAM'. Throughout this period, it is imperative to clear your mind of all distractions and focus solely on the root chakra and the manifestations it seeks to bring forth in your existence. It is recommended that you maintain this position and engage in slow, controlled breathing until a sensation of refreshment is experienced. An additional concept that numerous individuals have discovered effective when engaging in this activity involves visualizing a crimson blossom projecting powerful energy as they execute the exercise whilst maintaining their eyes shut.

The Third Eye Chakra
Third Eye Chakra Basics
T
The sixth chakra, known as the Third Eye chakra, resides in the frontal region of the cranium, precisely positioned above and amidst the eyebrows. The Sanskrit term for this chakra is Ajna, which may be interpreted as "perception" or "dominance." This energetic center pertains to our innate intuition, self-awareness, and transcendent insight. This chakra governs the pituitary and pineal glands, as well as the eyes and temples, with indigo being the color that is associated with it. The bija mantra associated with it is Om, phonetically pronounced as "ohm,"

and is the mantra that is widely recognized by the majority of individuals. According to belief, the sound "Om" holds the status of being the original sound of the Universe, serving as a powerful affirmation and recognized as the most significant of all mantras.

An Optimal State of the Third Eye Chakra
Maintaining the alignment of our Third Eye chakra enables us to remain connected to our innate intuition and instincts. Furthermore, it aids in the cultivation and sustenance of an elevated level of discernment, coupled with outstanding cognitive abilities.

Third Eye Chakra Imbalances

A scarcity of energy within the sixth chakra has the potential to impede our capacity to acknowledge or have faith in our intuition. It is possible that we may encounter difficulties in envisioning the future, exhibit limited creative thinking, experience heightened levels of stress, and manifest impaired memory function. An overabundance of energy within the Third Eye chakra may give rise to symptoms such as feelings of excessive apprehension, constant mental rumination, challenges in maintaining focus, and experiences of distressing dreams during sleep. From a physiological standpoint, we may experience sleep disruptions, sinus-related ailments, diminished visual acuity, migraines, depressive symptoms, or irregularities in hormonal levels.

Crystals & Stones

Gemstones of indigo, deep blue, and purple hues, particularly those that are linked to intuition, are suitable for incorporating into the practice of harmonizing the Third Eye chakra. Lapis lazuli, azurite, as well as labradorite, are among the stones that belong to this particular classification. When practicing meditation with a sufficiently small stone, it is possible to position it at the midpoint of the forehead when reclining. Larger stones can be easily grasped in one's palms while envisioning a state of equilibrium, receptiveness, and clarity within the Third Eye.

Foods & Herbs

There is a diverse range of nourishing foods that can support the well-being of the Third Eye chakra. These include fruits exhibiting a deep blue or purple hue, such as blackberries, raspberries, prunes, and purple grapes. Furthermore, we have the opportunity to savor assorted purple vegetables, including eggplant, purple cabbage, and purple onions. Another inclusion is dark chocolate, which has been demonstrated to aid in enhancing cognitive acuity. If one possesses an inclination towards utilizing herbs to enhance the functionality of their sixth chakra, the utilization of mugwort, lavender, and blue lotus may prove to be beneficial.

Essential Oils

Certain vital oils that could potentially assist in promoting the harmony and well-being of the

Third Eye chakra encompass yarrow, lemon, and sandalwood. These oils are conducive to the preservation of a serene and lucid state of mind.

7: The Chakra of Ultimate Enlightenment

The Crown Chakra, often referred to as our seventh and most elevated chakra, is prominently recognized. The activation of the Crown Chakra engenders a profound comprehension of the interconnectedness that exists between humanity and the cosmos, as well as our inherent unity with the divine. The Crown Chakra serves as the channel for us to tap into the sagacity and potency of our most authentic and elevated beings. Individuals who have successfully tapped into the energy of their Crown Chakra emanate sentiments of immense affection, enlightenment, and veracity.

Once the Crown Chakra is awakened, the integration of our ego with our spiritual essence is accomplished, establishing the necessary groundwork for the attainment of enlightenment. We are granted boundless opportunities to tap into a wealth of profound knowledge and imaginative drive, enabling us to unlock gateways to alternative realms and embark upon their exploration. We acquire the skills to integrate heightened states of awareness into our terrestrial existence, thereby transmuting all forms of energy into their utmost potentials. By attaining a direct alignment with the inherent energy present in the entirety of existence, we transition from a state of constant progression towards a state of steadfast existence.

Unimpeded access to the Crown Chakra bestows upon us boundless power and heightened perception, whereas its obstruction leads to a state of total immobilization. We forfeit our capacity for communication and decision-making, experiencing a complete absence of pleasure or joy. We experience a loss of self-identity and direction, while also impairing our capacity to perceive and actively engage with the broader aspects of life. We forfeit our adherence to our core principles and moral standards, succumbing to an egocentric mindset.

However, an excessive influx of energy from the Crown Chakra leads to a total lack of command. We perceive our own capabilities, yet struggle to ascertain the most effective means of harnessing and utilizing them. We experience immense distress, exhibiting various symptoms ranging from frequent migraines to manic-depressive episodes. Our emotional states fluctuate greatly between intense ardor and detachment, leading to a pronounced escalation in our actions, often resulting in harm.

The Crown Chakra is associated with the cranial region, the central nervous system, the glands responsible for secreting hormones such as the pineal and pituitary glands, and the integumentary and skeletal systems. An inequilibrium in the energy of this chakra can give rise to a range of physiological and psychological maladies. The most prevalent symptoms include heightened sensitivity to light and sound, as well as persistent fatigue.

An optimally functioning, well-aligned Crown Chakra facilitates our connection with divine guidance, providing us with access to the capacities of both the conscious and the subconscious mind. We acquire the ability to surpass the laws of nature and accomplish extraordinary feats. Deep within the Crown Chakra resides a profound comprehension of mortality and the eternal nature of our being. The Crown Chakra represents the attainment of enlightenment.

Indicators and Manifestations of Disruption in the Throat Chakra

The instances of physical imbalances comprise laryngitis, inflamed throats, thyroid disorders, ear infections, gastric ulcers, temporomandibular joint (TMJ) issues, shoulder discomfort, neck soreness, and any facial ailment.

Emotional maladies encompass difficulties pertaining to the articulation of thoughts and ideas both in written and verbal forms, lack of determination or resolve, apprehensions regarding the depletion of agency or influence, and perceiving a lack of command over one's own emotions and actions.

How to Achieve Equilibrium in Your Throat Chakra

When the Throat Chakra achieves equilibrium, the articulation of thoughts, the adherence to truth, and the facilitation of open and honest communication shall flow effortlessly. You will encounter no difficulty in expression and you will exhibit adeptness as an attentive listener.

Express Yourself Freely

Unfailingly endeavor to articulate your thoughts without inhibition through the acts of chanting, writing, singing, and transparently conveying your ideas. Please feel at liberty to independently craft unique content, such as composing original lyrics.

Utilize a Cervical Pillow for Relaxation

Tension is unfavorable for the Throat Chakra. Commence by indulging in the relaxation of your jaw, subsequently initiating a gradual and unhurried movement of your head and neck, alternating from left to right. Perform this action on multiple occasions. After completing your task, proceed to gently massage the nape of your neck while inhaling deeply a few times.

It's Yoga Time

Once more, it is advisable to engage in the practice of yoga in order to facilitate the establishment of equilibrium within a chakra. Endeavor to incorporate yoga into your daily regimen to effectively obtain the utmost advantages concerning the harmonization of the chakras. The Fish pose is regarded as a beneficial yoga posture for the activation of the Throat Chakra.

Begin by assuming a supine position. Please straighten your leg and place your arms by your sides, with your palms facing downwards. While applying pressure to your forearms and elbows against the floor, elevate your chest to generate a pronounced curvature in your upper back. Ensure the maintenance of exerted pressure on your hands and forearms, while simultaneouly maintaining the activation and energy in your thighs.

Create a Manifestation Journal

Devote a portion of each day to meticulously documenting your objectives and aspirations. One should refrain from passing judgment upon oneself or engaging in self-censorship of one's thoughts. Simply record your thoughts on paper – you may be pleasantly surprised by the manifestations that can occur as a result, aiding in the maintenance of a clear Throat Chakra.

Use Essential Oils

Utilize the properties of essential oils. They possess the capacity to effectively restore equilibrium to your chakra system. Add a single drop of each Neroli, Sandalwood, and Lavender into carrier oil, followed by a delicate application of the mixture onto the neck through gentle massage.

Use Healing Affirmations

Utilizing therapeutic affirmations proves to be an effective approach in purifying and harmonizing the energy flow of your Throat Chakra. A demonstration of an assertion could be stated as follows: "I willingly and exuberantly articulate my true self." I exhibit assuredness and fluency in my speech, displaying an unrestrained willingness to express my creative ideas. I adhere to my personal beliefs and remain receptive to the prospect of change."

The Heart Chakra

While there may be a loose association with love, the essence of this is unequivocally centered around the concept of love. The connection is not tenuous with love, nor does it pertain to the heart as a vital organ. It resides superior to the heart, serving as the epitome from which love originates.

Unblocking a Sacral Blockage

This particular chakra issue can pose significant challenges, as it necessitates a requisite level of self-acceptance and comprehensiveness in its resolution.

This poses a challenge for the majority of individuals, but it presents an even greater struggle for those experiencing the consequences of sacral blockage. Indeed, the challenge of addressing emotional concerns surpasses that of dealing with physical ailments.

The initial stage entails directly addressing and acknowledging your concerns. It is imperative that you cultivate the ability to refrain from suppressing the discomfort that you are attempting to disregard, and instead permit yourself to fully undergo its effects.

Cease the suppression of negative memories and emotions; it is imperative for you to cultivate trust in your emotional state. Once you have developed a deeper familiarity with this subject matter, you will acquire the ability to comprehend the fundamental causes of your issues and formulate potential strategies to resolve them.

There exists invariably a solution to overcome your difficulties, albeit it will require your utmost resolve and determination to attain it. It may be necessary to seek assistance from external sources as well. Severe eating disorders pose a significant threat to health and necessitate professional medical intervention for successful recovery.

Water can prove to be a valuable ally amidst the challenges encountered in this arduous journey. It fails to address the fundamental underlying concerns, yet it can provide solace and promote relaxation as you actively engage in resolving these concerns.

Immersing oneself in warm baths, whether infused with orange essential oils or without, can potentially elicit favorable influences on the sacral chakra. Additionally, indulging in a warm bath can effectively induce relaxation and serve as a gentle reminder to approach this arduous task with a more measured and patient mindset.

Additionally, engaging in alternative aquatic endeavors, such as swimming, could prove beneficial. Venturing to the seaside or the nearby aquatic facility is worth experimenting with. It has the potential to significantly impact your emotional state.

Citrus-based beverages and foods may also assist in relieving a sacral blockage, although their effects will be limited to surface-level relief. Water and color may provide assistance, but genuine success can only be achieved through a willingness to directly address and diligently resolve one's problems.

BALANCING THE CHAKRAS

When endeavoring to acquire knowledge on the methods of Chakra balancing, one may inquire about the means by which all the chakras can be harmonized, considering that the rationale behind this necessity has already been communicated to them. In this section, you will gain insight into the current state or condition of your chakras, prior to commencing any efforts towards their healing. You will also gain knowledge regarding the paramount importance of achieving chakra equilibrium. Upon completion of this , you will possess the capability to discern instances wherein your chakras have succumbed to an imbalance.

Let us commence by gaining comprehension of the various states exhibited by the chakras.

Distinct states of the Chakra system" "Varied circumstances affecting the Chakra" "Diverse scenarios impacting the Chakra" "Various manifestations of the Chakra's condition

Previously, you were informed that the chakras are commonly referred to as the wheels of life, highlighting the concept that these chakras are perpetually imbued with luminosity. There will come a moment when the luminosity of this light will commence to diminish substantially. It is crucial to possess comprehension of the present state of the chakras to prevent any potential complications going forward. It is imperative that you acquire a comprehensive understanding of how the energy circulates within your physiological system. If there happens to be an individual present in your vicinity possessing the ability to perceive Auras, it is highly probable that they would observe the energies encircling you manifesting a phenomenon akin to a swirling vortex. This vortex pertains to your chakra, which is located within seven distinct regions of your body. You will observe the presence of a vortex in both the anterior and posterior regions surrounding your chakras. This assertion does not hold true in the context of the crown chakra.

Gaining knowledge about the states of the chakra

It is imperative to comprehend the stages of the chakras as they hold utmost significance. You will gain comprehension of the appropriate healing technique to employ solely upon recognizing the states of the chakras. Within this segment, you will acquire knowledge about the techniques for discerning the various states of your chakras, thereby facilitating their subsequent healing.

The Open State

When situated within a reverent environment dedicated to healing, you will discover your capacity to initiate their healing process. During this particular phase, the chakras remain receptive to acquiring the requisite energy. When the chakra is in this condition, one will observe an unobstructed flow of energy emanating from the chakra, circulating within the surrounding environment, and returning back into the chakra. While occupying the hallowed and restorative surroundings, your chakras will experience heightened receptivity compared to their usual state. Prior to commencing the session devoted to chakra healing, it is imperative that you initiate the process of opening your chakras.

The Blocked State

It has been communicated to you that the chakras consistently possess swirling energy within them. This energy manifests as light, and in the event that the chakra becomes obstructed, the light's rotation will become disrupted, ceasing to follow its original course and starting to move in a reversed direction. In the event that there is an obstruction in one chakra, it can be observed that the remaining chakras become obstructed in a similar manner. This phenomenon can be attributed to the absence of any flow of energy within the chakras. In the process of chakra healing, it is necessary to employ the inherent energy within the respective chakra in order to restore and harmonize its function.

The Sealed State

The chakras are all encompassed by a protective layer that functions as a barrier. This is the one that guarantees optimal functioning of all the chakras. They also assess the sufficiency of energy within the chakra and take note of whether or not it necessitates acquiring energy from the cosmos. After completing the process of chakra healing, it is imperative to undertake the task of closing or sealing the chakras.

The Therapeutic and Harmonized Chakras

This represents the optimal state achieved by the chakra following complete healing process. Upon the successful restoration of the chakras, they will attain uniformity in terms of their dimensions. Sufficient energy will be present in the chakras at this point, given that you have recently completed the healing process. After complete healing, the energy shall effortlessly traverse through the chakras. You will come to the realization that they do not necessitate any additional energy whatsoever. This would imply that the chakras would commence rotation in the appropriate manner. There exists a multitude of diverse assertions regarding the rotational patterns of the chakras. There are those who subscribe to the notion that the chakras rotate in a clockwise manner, whereas there exists another camp of individuals who maintain that the chakras rotate in a counterclockwise direction. It is advisable to consider the notion that your chakras exhibit a clockwise spinning motion when in a state of balance, and conversely, rotate in the opposite direction when experiencing an imbalance.

Your Root at Work

The workplace or professional setting provides an excellent opportunity to integrate Chakras, particularly the Root

Chakra. The everyday pressures of meeting deadlines, difficulties encountered with assignments, and interpersonal challenges with colleagues possess the capacity to disturb our state of composure. When these adverse emotions prompt us to doubt our choices or feel remorse for our behaviors, we erode fragments of our psychological equilibrium and disturb the harmony within ourselves. Maintaining awareness of our fundamental principles at the workplace provides a solution to this issue. "Upon experiencing these sensations, we recommend implementing the following strategies:

Rooted Feet

1.) In instances where you feel the initial signs of stress, frustration, or irritation towards yourself or your colleagues in a professional setting, it is essential to recall and reflect upon your fundamental guiding principle or core values.

2.) Whilst engaging in deliberate and controlled respiration, visualize your Root chakra releasing detrimental energy and incorporating solely affirmative energy.

3.) While facing demanding circumstances or individuals, it is important to recognize the sensation of contact between your feet and the ground and allow a profound sense of stability to permeate your being.

Ensuring a steadfast connection to your workplace environment will facilitate emotional regulation, cognitive stability, and overall preservation of your well-being.

Sacral Chakra | Svadhishthana

The awakening of the Sacral chakra...

The crystals in question are moonstone, citrine, coral, aventurine, agate, and calcite.

Botanical Extracts - Aniba rosaeodora, Salvia officinalis, Pogostemon cablin

Audio - Fundamental note: D, frequency: 288 Hz, Sounds of ocean, rainfall, and waterfall, Chant mantra: Vam.

Nutrition sources include various types of food such as fats and oils, tropical fruits, fish and seafood, nuts and seeds, fermented foods, almonds, papaya, melon, passion fruit, pumpkin, orange, coconut, mandarins, mangos, walnuts, and melon.

Yoga Postures - cobra pose, triangle pose, lord of the dance pose, butterfly pose

Governs - Regulates, influences, governs, oversees, supervises, controls, manages, orchestrates, directs, presides over, administers, guides - Movement, flow, creativity, relationships, emotions, sensuality, monetary matters, lower back, pelvis, fertility, bladder.

I perceive plentifulness in every direction, both within and encircling me.

Do you possess a favorable rapport with financial matters? Do you encounter difficulties when it comes to relationships with individuals? Are you experiencing a state of creative stagnation? If that is the case, it would be advisable for you to devote attention to cultivating your Sacral chakra. This particular chakra possesses great strength and is frequently overlooked and misconstrued. The considerable financial resources dedicated annually to fertility treatments could be effectively conserved if individuals facing fertility challenges prioritized the cultivation of their Sacral chakra prior to resorting to pharmaceutical interventions. This can present itself anatomically as abdominal pain, a urinary tract infection, a fungal infection or a more severe medical condition. Do not overlook the inherent potential encapsulated within this chakra. In the event that your Sacral chakra is blocked, you will experience a disconnection from your emotional state. You will not experience a sense of physical comfort and well-being. Emotions and sexual expression are integral components of the human experience.

The Sacral chakra facilitates the utilization of one's soul's true calling and vitality in order to manifest one's own affluence and wealth. It facilitates an enjoyable and imaginative experience throughout the entirety of the process. If your intention is to manifest something previously unknown, it is imperative to focus your attention on this particular chakra.

I derive great pleasure from crafting a refreshing fruit medley with tropical flavors as I focus on nurturing and balancing my Sacral chakra. The ingredients that will be incorporated comprise pineapple, papaya, coconut, almonds, walnuts, passion fruit, mandarins, and sunflower seeds. If you so desire, you may also incorporate dried fruit to create a trail mix comprising comparable components. This is the exclusive method by which my husband will consume this mixture. He thoroughly enjoys consuming this particular food item during his mountain treks. In addition, we have a fondness for utilizing the burning of sage when we experience a sense of disconnection from our Sacral chakras. We are fortunate to have an abundance of wild sage in our vicinity, and acquiring smudge sticks is a readily available option. Sage possesses strong purifying properties that effectively cleanse and balance your Sacral chakra. Furthermore, should you choose to incorporate orange oil into your household cleaning routine. The incorporation of orange peels into vinegar to effectively cleanse windows presents itself as a commendable technique in aiding the purification of one's Sacral chakra. The act of cleansing these windows with the color orange will facilitate the unblocking of your sacral chakra, as your perspective of the world is influenced through these windows. Indeed, should one possess the opportunity to access a waterfall, engaging in the act of playing within the cascading waters would undeniably stand as a tremendously potent means to activate and awaken one's Sacral chakra. Our waterfalls are exclusively accessible during the summer season, as the glacial melt remains exceptionally frigid, even amidst warm temperatures. During the winter we will climb on top of the frozen waterfall. Although it may not provide the same level of assistance as engaging in aquatic activities at the waterfall, it is certainly an enjoyable experience.

Solar Plexus Chakra, also known as Manipura: "The Third Chakra, the Solar Plexus Chakra, commonly referred to as Manipura:

I do.

मणिपूर

Third Chakra: Situated beneath the solar plexus

Color - Yellow

Element - Fire

Word - Self-esteem

The activation of the Solar Plexus chakra...

Crystalline specimens - Golden calcite, topaz, citrine, amber

Botanical extracts - Fennel, juniperberry, lemongrass

Sound - keynote: E, frequency: 320 Hz, crackling fire, sacred chant: Ram.

Food items - Sources of carbohydrates, nutritious sweeteners, soluble dietary fiber, pulses, whole grains, warming herbs and spices, maize, pineapples, gourds, legumes, bell peppers, bananas, oats, quinoa, ginger, turmeric.

Yoga Asanas - dhanurasana, navasana, setu bandhasana, ardha matsyendrasana

Governs - Regulation of digestion, body weight, kidney function, managing addictive tendencies, enhancement of self-worth, accountability, professional endeavors, strong determination, maintaining equilibrium, consistent energy levels, fostering personal growth, fostering confidence, and influence.

"I do enough."

The Solar Plexus chakra governs one's personal power. If you experience significant distress or a sensation of breathlessness, it is advisable to focus on the cultivation of the Solar Plexus chakra. This is the domain in which we retain our authority, self-importance, and determination. If one allows oneself to be easily manipulated when confronted with a locked situation, it is indicative of being easily controlled by others. It also governs one's sense of personal safety and comfort when it comes to being observed. When the Solar Plexus chakra becomes blocked, it gives rise to heightened difficulties. Nevertheless, in the event that it becomes excessively active, one may exhibit an overwhelming demeanor and a sense of grandiosity. We require the capability to generate and exert a significant impact. Please accept this blueprint as a symbol of peace and generosity. If one harbors numerous constraining beliefs, embracing the activation of their Solar Plexus chakra would undeniably prove advantageous. Difficulties may overcome us, yet trials promote our strength. Occasionally, altering one's lexicon can yield considerable efficacy. By accessing and opening your Solar Plexus, you will create space for the expansion of your personal energy, enabling you to engage in actions that extend beyond your own needs.

By dedicating your efforts towards the development of the Solar Plexus, you are bestowing upon the world the essence of your being. Many individuals adhering to a carbohydrate-free diet may discover that their Solar Plexus chakra becomes blocked. An effective method to awaken this chakra is to engage in rhythmic movement while encircling a blazing fire. If you do not have an inclination towards dancing, you may opt to socialize in the vicinity of the fire instead. Observing and attentively listening to a fire holds tremendous potential in unlocking this specific chakra, particularly when practiced during the nighttime hours. Exposure to sunlight is also highly beneficial for the activation and harmonization of the Solar Plexus chakra. For approximately 15 minutes, engage in the practice of envisioning the sun's rays being directed towards your Solar Plexus chakra in a focused manner.

Indications of an Impaired Throat Chakra

There exist numerous indications associated with the impaired state of the throat chakras, and a significant portion of these manifestations are of a physical nature. The occurrence of headaches, fatigue, or a sore throat may be indicative of an obstructed throat chakra.

Listed below are several frequently observed symptoms:

Sore Throat

It may appear somewhat paradoxical, yet concurrently, quite appropriate that a hoarse throat would coincide with a compromised throat chakra. It appears that the sensation of a lump in your throat, resulting from a multitude of unresolved conflicts, can potentially develop into an obstruction of your throat chakra on an ethereal level. The throat chakra is correlated with the anatomical regions encompassing the throat, sinuses, oral cavity, mandible, and the glandular structure of the thyroid. Should you encounter difficulty with any of these, it may potentially indicate an underlying concern pertaining to the throat chakra.

Asthma

The manifestation of asthma can be observed as a consequence of an impaired throat chakra. Similarly, the constrained flow of energy correlates with an impeded respiratory function, resulting in intensified physical discomfort during breathing. Coincidentally, it has been discovered that the utilization of respiratory techniques has proven to be quite effective in addressing not only asthma but also a constricted throat chakra. Should you perceive a sensation of constriction and blockage in your throat chakra, it is possible that the method to unlock it lies in the simple action of engaging in a few deep, mindful breaths.

Fatigue

The obstruction of the throat chakra may result in persistent exhaustion. Living with such a burden on one's central means of communication and expression can be incredibly tiresome and draining. Every instance in which you experience a sense of stiflement or oppression as an individual will inevitably incur a toll upon your well-being, ultimately leading to a state of utter exhaustion over time.

Anemia

Anemia is reputed to arise from insufficient iron levels in the bloodstream; moreover, it can potentially be initiated by an imbalanced throat chakra. An imbalanced throat chakra can result in systemic disharmony within the entire body. An individual exhibiting such imbalances in their chakric system may experience physical manifestations, such as the development of anemia.

Apprehension towards engaging in open dialogue

For an individual exhibiting an obstructed throat chakra, engaging in open discourse can be a source of trepidation. They have completely lost confidence in their own verbal expression and public speaking skills, resulting in significant anxiety when faced with the need to engage in such activities. If you experience a level of apprehension that surpasses the typical nervousness associated with being on stage, it is possible that this heightened fear is linked to an obstructed throat chakra.

Challenging Articulation

Individuals who are afflicted by an obstructed throat chakra may encounter challenges when it comes to articulating their thoughts and emotions. They may encounter difficulty in locating suitable verbiage as their capacity for creative expression, specifically their throat chakra, has been effectively hindered. It is imperative to ensure the continual openness and upkeep of the throat chakra in order to facilitate the manifestation of efficacious freedom of expression.

Feeling Misunderstood

Individuals who experience an obstructed throat chakra tend to have an underlying sense of being misunderstood. When the throat chakra is operating optimally, it instills within us a sense of social interconnectedness and instills within us a sense of self-assurance in our own innate gifts and capabilities. However, when there is an obstruction in the throat chakra, it is not uncommon to experience a sense of utter inadequacy in articulating our thoughts and emotions effectively, and a prevailing belief that our true essence is not truly comprehended by others.

Allowing Others to Take Charge of the Conversation

An obstruction of the throat chakra may result in timidity, rendering it exceedingly difficult for those affected to take the lead in a conversation. Individuals experiencing a blocked throat chakra frequently encounter the inclination to relinquish conversational control to others. To liberate oneself from these limitations, it is necessary to unlock the throat chakra.

Exhibiting a strong aversion to confrontation "

Excessive confrontational behavior should be avoided, as evidenced by frequent news reports highlighting the negative consequences of individuals displaying an overly confrontational attitude. However, an equally detrimental outcome can result from the opposite extreme. An individual who adamantly avoids and abstains from engaging in any form of confrontation is prone to allowing others to exert dominance over them, consistently suppressing their own ability to express themselves and present their own perspective. And individuals who experience an imbalance in their throat chakra may exhibit such an excessive aversion to confrontation that they permit others to exploit or dominate them.

Lightheadedness

An impairment in the function of the throat chakra may result in sensations of dizziness. These sensations of vulnerability arise from the diminished potency of the throat chakra. If you are experiencing symptoms of dizziness, it is advisable to consider the condition of your throat chakra.

2

Restoring Your Soul

It is likely that you have encountered individuals who claim that we possess the capacity to facilitate our own healing. Seems pretty farfetched, right? Where would one commence the process for this endeavor? However, it is widely acknowledged that the mind possesses immense power, although one may not be fully cognizant of its entire potential. You just, know. Yes? Through extensive therapeutic intervention, including extensive participation in talk show therapy, we have acquired a profound understanding over the course of several years regarding the profound impact of pessimistic thoughts on our mental, physical, and spiritual well-being. Negative thoughts or words, once internalized and embraced, have the power to shape our beliefs and manifest themselves in our reality. This is the method by which perpetrators maintain dominance over their targets. One easily starts to internalize the words spoken, be it one's own statements or those of others. Hence, it is imperative to cultivate the ability to release these thoughts on a daily basis. The profound influence on various aspects of your existence, including your self-worth and inner being, is immense, constituting a significant impediment to the realization of your aspirations.

The practical activity that was undertaken in one with the intention of establishing a solid foundation for you is commendable. It is imperative that you make a deliberate decision to relinquish detrimental and deleterious thoughts. An individual trapped in the clutches of addiction is profoundly hindered by this entrapment within their psyche, lacking the necessary means to liberate themselves from their internal confinement. Many individuals form judgments about them, perceiving them as lacking discipline. Contemplate this though. If it were within our collective ability to manifest wellness through sheer determination, we would all inhabit a state of robust health, resounding success, and profound contentment. In all candor, it is not as straightforward as it may seem.

Nevertheless, we can engage in the implementation of mindfulness techniques, meditation practices, energy healing sessions, and the exploration of our individual talents. We can acquire the ability to relinquish our attachments, for in the broader context, we excessively concern ourselves with matters that are truly inconsequential. Consider the instance wherein a dear individual encounters injury, though you subsequently ascertain that their condition is slated for recovery. Life becomes crystal clear, and one realizes that the essence of existence lies in loving one another to the fullest extent possible while leading a fulfilling and joyous life. Undoubtedly, articulating these concepts poses little challenge, while implementing them entails significantly greater difficulty. It appears to be relatively effortless for me to compose these words of encouragement addressed to you. I kindly request that you make an effort to acquaint yourself with these techniques, direct your attention towards cultivating mindfulness and the ability to reside in the present moment, and, as it is commonly expressed, refrain from excessively worrying about trivial matters.

Guided Meditation for the Balancing and Restoration of Chakras (Duration: 20 – 30 minutes)

Assume a comfortable, upright position and place your hands delicately in your lap.

Bear in mind, you possess the capacity to restore and rejuvenate your existence.

Henceforth, with each inhalation, you invite an untainted luminosity, an ethereal therapeutic force that permeates your being, instilling within you a rejuvenating serenity and invigorating vitality that has long eluded you.

With each exhalation, one dispels the concerns, stress, and pessimism that have been harbored within their being. Let it go. It is okay.

You will not be harmed.

Your space, your mind, body, and soul are exclusively receptive to goodness and light.

Close your eyes, inhale deeply, and release a slow exhale, allowing yourself to attain a state of tranquil composure.

As one engages in the act of exhalation, a discernible sensation arises - the release of tension, accompanied by the departure of bothersome thoughts, all transpiring through the expulsion of one's breath.

Inhale deeply, allowing the infusion of curative white radiance into your being.

Breathe out gradually, expelling your concerns, negative thoughts, and sorrow, releasing them downwards into the soil for purification.

Inhale deeply, allowing the soothing white light to permeate your being with each breath.

Allow your physical being to relinquish all accumulated tension.

Exhale, expelling any concerns accumulated over the course of the day, releasing them into the distance.

Experience the soothing sensation of your muscles unwinding with each therapeutic inhalation.

Please inhale, consciously perceiving your surroundings.

Take note of the auditory and olfactory sensations. The illumination emanating from within the closed cavities of your eyes.

You are merging harmoniously with the surrounding space.

Inhale and exhale gradually, sensing the gentle expansion and contraction of your thoracic region.

Allow your mind to find tranquility, and should thoughts arise, acknowledge them and promptly let them go, just as swiftly as they entered your consciousness.

You have no worries.

You are in a state of safety, comfort, and protection.

You have no worries.

You are in a state of ensured safety, comfort, and protection.

Direct your breath downwards, towards the foundation of your physical being.

Inhale deeply, directing your breath towards the root chakra, situated beneath the lowermost part of your spinal column.

With each inhalation, you imbibe a pristine luminosity that bestows healing upon you.

Allow your chakra to gradually relax and broaden as you inhale, thereby providing sustenance and vital energy to your root chakra.

Imagine a harmonious and vitalizing bond between your foundational chakra and the fertile and curative terrestrial ground.

Envision your base chakra, an illuminated crimson core of energy that anchors you, fortifying you in the present moment.

Permit your foundational structure to acquire its necessary sustenance.

I am readily embraced for who I am.

'I am supported.'

Inhale deeply, exhale gradually.

Direct your attention to your sacral chakra, situated beneath your navel, which serves as the focal point for your emotional intelligence, decision-making abilities, artistic expression, enjoyment, and vitality.

Sense the inhalation and exhalation envelop this space.

Allow it to soften and elongate as you exhale, allowing your sacral chakra to receive sustenance and vital life energy.

In your mental imagery, an incandescent orange core materializes, resembling the hue of a descending sun, instilling equilibrium, fortitude, and inspiration within you.

I hold my needs in high regard.

I grant myself the opportunity to receive sustenance.

Breathe in again. Heal.

Breathe out again. Release yourself from all sources of pain and distress.

Healing breaths in.

Pain and concern dissipate.

Direct your focus to the region beneath your sternum, specifically the area known as the solar plexus. This represents the locus of your personal power.

Inhale deeply, allowing your solar plexus to relax, and visualize a radiant yellow glow, reminiscent of the brilliance of sunlight.

Breathe out.

Immerse your solar plexus in the radiant rays of sunlight, rejuvenating, replenishing, and providing essential nourishment to allow your chakra to absorb its requisite energy.

'I value myself.'

'I am enough.'

I possess an abundance of capabilities.

Inhale deeply into your abdominal region once more, and proceed to exhale fully.

Direct your attention to the central area of your chest, specifically to your cardiac region. Your intrinsic energy flow associated with personal growth and boundless affection.

Inhale softly and deeply, allowing the breath to penetrate your heart center.

Allow it to soften and expand as you exhale.

Request the presence of a vivid emerald-hued illumination, a captivating manifestation of the vibrant season of spring.

Envelop your heart with sustenance, rejuvenation, and restoration, allowing it to acquire the necessary nourishment.

I am deeply cherished.

I grant myself the freedom to express and receive love without restraint.

I derive sustenance from the formidable force of affection.

Inhale deeply, followed by a deliberate exhalation.

Direct your attention towards your neck area, specifically your throat region, and specifically focus on the chakra associated with personal determination and assertiveness.

Inhale deeply, allowing your throat chakra to relax and widen.

Imagine a lucid azure ring of radiance, akin to the celestial heavens.

Inhale the restorative radiance into your laryngeal region, gently easing, expanding, and liberating your capacity for self-articulation and innovation.

Allow your throat chakra to receive and absorb what is necessary for its well-being. Nourishment, renewal, healing.

I acknowledge and express my personal truth.

I articulate my thoughts without inhibition.

I grant myself the privilege of expressing my opinions.

Deep breath in. And out.

Direct your attention to the center of your forehead, the space between your eyebrows, and your third eye area.

Your reservoir of wisdom and intuitive faculties.

As you inhale, you conscientiously permit it to relax, enlarge, and respire.

One observes a lively indigo hue, reminiscent of the velvety shade that graces the nocturnal sky.

Immerse your spiritual consciousness in a circular spectrum of indigo, promoting equilibrium, tranquility, and cultivating profound discernment, comprehension, and clarity.

Allow your third eye to acquire what is necessary. Nourishment, renewal, healing.

All events are transpiring according to their destined course.

Inhale deeply once more.

And out again.

Please proceed upwards, to the highest point of your head, where your crown chakra is located.

Gradually, in a gentle glow, delicately immerse yourself in the aura surrounding your head. Bringing about equilibrium and fostering harmony.

Allow your tiara to extract the necessary benefits from the therapeutic services you are rendering.

Nourishment, renewal, healing.

I am unified with all aspects of existence and all individuals.

I am deeply interconnected with the cosmos.

Breathe in fully.

Exhale fully.

Now.

Feel your full body. As though you had merged seamlessly with your own skin.

Sensating the complete contour of your physique.

It is possible that you are experiencing the release of a reservoir of pent-up energy.

Employing deliberate focus and mindful attention, channel this energy towards your abdominal region for the purpose of accumulation. You may access this resource as needed.

Prior to concluding this meditation session, please allocate a brief duration of time to tenderly and benevolently acknowledge the extraordinary and exquisite essence that comprises your being.

Inhale deeply one final time for the purpose of restoring your well-being. And at this juncture, you may release it.

HEALING THE THIRD CHAKRA

The solar plexus, also known as Manipura, is the third chakra situated at the lower torso, precisely at the intersection of the rib cage and the upper abdomen. Its symbolic identity is attributed to the vibrant hue of yellow. This particular chakra is frequently linked with avian symbolism and the act of flying, as it serves as the initial gateway enabling us to venture beyond our ethereal being and establish connections with various beings, locations, and entities. From a physiological standpoint, this particular chakra is linked to the muscular system, the gastrointestinal tract, our overall metabolic functioning, as well as our neural network.

In order to grasp the concept of the third chakra fully, it is imperative to acknowledge that it occupies a superior position in relation to the two foundational chakras, often referred to as the "survival" chakras, primarily concerned with one's individual self. The third chakra pertains to the concept of self-acceptance, personal assurance, and our capacity to establish meaningful connections with others. It represents a departure from self-indulgence and concerns solely focused on personal pleasure and survival, and a shift towards fostering a sense of community and cultivating meaningful relationships.

When the third chakra is efficiently regulated, we experience a sense of ease in our aptitude to establish connections with others and demonstrate proficient self-organization. When an obstruction or imbalance occurs in this chakra, it gives rise to significant issues in our capacity to effectively collaborate within a team or perform proficiently in any collective circumstance. This can be perceived in the form of challenges in managing hierarchical structures, a struggle to establish connections with others, as well as feelings of anger and frustration.

In essence, this chakra serves to govern our self-assurance and self-assurance in our interactions as members of society. When experiencing discontent or dissatisfaction with ourselves, it follows naturally that our ability to connect with others and foster resentment is diminished.

Associated fragrances: Marigold, cinnamon, and carnation

Herbs with a connection: Lemon balm and goldenseal

Glandular systems in conjunction: The gallbladder, liver, and spleen

Musical note: E

Chakra phonetic representation: The vowel sound 'O' pronounced like in the words top, pop, or dollop.

Element: Fire

Healing crystals: Golden topaz, tiger's eye, amber, calcite of gold, unadulterated gold, and citrine.

Color: Yellow

Healing exercises:
Kundalini yoga, particularly emphasizing the boat pose.

Performing rhythmic bodily movements, particularly involving swaying and undulating motions, particularly in the area of the pelvis.

Healing foods:

Any items that possess a yellow hue, such as corn, split peas, and certain types of beans.

Examples of grains and fiber include whole wheat, granola, or whole grain varieties.

Herbal infusions with a gentle taste, especially those infused with peppermint and mint leaves.

Seven: Restoring Balance to the Fourth Chakra

The fourth chakra, known as the Anahata or heart chakra, resides in the precise middle section of the chest, situated around the vicinity of the heart and slightly above it. It is exemplified by mammals and the human existence, and is intricately linked to the emotional core and our sentiments. It is likely that you have already observed the correlation between the lower chakras and the self, be it in terms of our primal emotions and associations, progressing towards our sense of contentment, personal growth, and assertiveness, and extending further towards genuine expressions of care, attachment, and empathy towards others.

The influence of our fourth chakra extends to our interpersonal connections and interactions with other entities in the world, encompassing both feelings of joy and acceptance as well as those of pain and fear. Therefore, it governs our relationship with the natural world, the botanical realm, and our immediate and extended kin. The heart chakra is the source of the renowned 'Christ energy,' encompassing our unwavering acceptance and delight in others. The sentiments linked to this chakra encompass compassion, love, forgiveness, empathy, trust, our state of emotional balance, and a sense of harmony with existence. If our heart chakra is robust, we may experience a profound inclination towards endeavors of a humanitarian nature.

If there is an imbalance or disruption in the state of the heart chakra, it is possible for us to experience physical ailments such as respiratory or pulmonary issues, as well as conditions related to the cardiovascular system like heartburn or other disorders. The primary manifestation of issues concerning this particular chakra, nonetheless, manifests in emotional distress, melancholy, and a prevailing sense of inner void. The presence of challenges pertaining to affection, encompassing sentiments of inadequacy, lack of affection, or emotional volatility, can be attributed to the activation of this particular chakra.

Associated fragrances: Lavender, yarrow, orris root, jasmine, meadowsweet, and marjoram.

Herbs typically found in association: Rue and saffron

Related glandular system: Thymus

Musical note: F

Phonetic representation of the chakra sound: 'A' as in distant, remote, and automobile.

Element: Air

The following gemstones are included: green jade, green aventurine, emerald, malachite, fluorite, ruby, moldavite, kunzite,

rose quartz, chrysoprase, and pink tourmaline.
Color: Green or gold

Healing exercises:
Bikram yoga
Sufi heart practices focusing on the acceptance and cultivation of love.
Sun salutation (yoga)

4: Fundamental Methods for Enhancing Chakra Levels

There exist a plethora of uncomplicated (yet advantageous!) methodologies that you can employ to enhance the energetic circulation in the seven therapeutic focal points of your physical being. These techniques are aesthetically pleasing, impart a sense of therapeutic and calming effects, and serve as effective mechanisms for stress reduction. Stress poses significant detrimental effects to the body's healing mechanisms and may progressively manifest in physical symptoms. These exercises are effective in mitigating stress, thereby contributing significantly to the enhancement of your chakras.

MEDITATION

Meditation promotes overall wellness by positively impacting the entirety of your being, encompassing physical, mental, and spiritual aspects. It facilitates tranquility of the mind, fostering an innate sense of serenity.

Curative Exercises Targeting Individual Chakras:

These exercises encompass effective methods for augmenting the vitality of each individual chakra, thereby facilitating the restoration of equilibrium within these therapeutic focal points.

Root Chakra Exercise:

Engaging in physical activity is the optimal method for fostering long-term healing of the root chakra, as this chakra is closely interconnected with the physicality of one's being. Engaging in the practice of hatha yoga proves to be highly advantageous for the stabilization and enhancement of this particular energy center. An alternate therapeutic approach that is highly conducive to the stimulation of the root chakra is aromatherapy, as this particular chakra is intricately connected to olfaction.

Sacral Chakra Exercise:

In addition, this particular chakra can receive advantageous effects from engaging in physical pursuits such as hatha yoga, specifically embracing tantric-oriented yoga practices that explore matters of intimacy. Aquatic pursuits such as swimming and watsu are of particular merit, given that this chakra is intricately associated with the properties of the water element.

Solar Plexus Chakra Exercise:

The utilization of visual exercises, such as yantra, proves advantageous to the optimization of this energy center. Engaging in sun exposure (with adequate application of sunscreen) can significantly contribute to the nourishment of this chakra, given its association with the fire element and its position in the solar plexus. Furthermore, should you be inclined, engaging in the act of fire-walking can be regarded as a profoundly efficacious means of fortifying and enhancing the solar plexus chakra.

Heart Chakra Exercise:

Physical contact provides a highly effective therapeutic modality for addressing the imbalances in this specific energy center. It is evident that physical embrace is fundamental for the well-being of individuals. Engaging in hugging, including self-affectionate gestures, represents a straightforward and remarkably impactful therapeutic technique to fortify and enhance the heart chakra. Additionally, employing Emotional Freedom Techniques (EFT), a practice centered around tapping, serves as a commendable endeavor to promote the vitality of the heart chakra.

Throat Chakra Exercise:

Sound healing can be an effective remedy for this particular situation. There exist a pair of uncomplicated methods for employing this technique. The initial approach entails emitting sound through various means, such as chanting, employing mantras or seed sounds, or simply vocalizing a beloved song. Alternatively, one can employ the technique of generating sound. Sound can be eliminated through the utilization of crystal bowls, recitation of mantras, or alternatively, by listening to a preferred musical composition.

Presented below are the seed sounds, also known as the shortest mantras, designated for every chakra, which represents each individual energy center:

- 1st - Lam

- 2nd - Vam

- 3rd - Ram

- 4th - Yam

- 5th - Ham

- Sixth - Om

- Seventh - Tranquil stillness (undeniable awareness)

The most effective means by which to engage the sixth chakra, commonly known as the Third Eye chakra, is through the practice of visualization, as it is through this channel that our aspirations and imagery materialize within the expanse of our mind's eye.

The Crown chakra can be enhanced through the practice of meditation, characterized by a state of pure, profound serenity and a profound absence of thoughts.

INDICATIONS OF CHAKRA UNDERACTIVITY:
You operate within a familiar environment that allows minimal opportunities for innovation.

Due to the presence of more pressing matters, you no longer engage in recreational activities.

Your artistic imagination is concealed by a pragmatic inventory (similar to desire)

You are experiencing frequent episodes of urinary tract infections, alternatively accompanied by discomfort in the lower back.

Everything is planned. Spontaneity has no place.

On the other hand, the indications of an excessively active sacred chakra:

Seeking satisfaction above all else, akin to an irresistible craving

The unfamiliar exerts a magnetic pull on your curiosity: a novel realm.

You neglect the essential necessities in order to engage in frivolous activities.

You amass triumphs on the Internet, in the physical realm, or in both domains.

You may also opt to take our test at this location in order to determine the state of your sacred chakra.

How can one restore equilibrium to their sacred chakra?

Meditation serves as a noble pathway towards attaining equilibrium. It may appear paradoxical, but as our life becomes increasingly bustling with labor, commitments, and limitations, the necessity for meditation grows more imperative. Giving priority to the act of calmly visualizing the radiance of your energy centers with their respective hues, while our world continues to be engulfed in chaos and foolishness, is imperative.

The sacred chakra is represented by the mantra VAM (please refer to our article on mantras for more information). This sound will facilitate the harmonization of this energy center.

All yoga asanas that facilitate the hip-opening process (such as the butterfly pose) are equally effective for the purpose of unblocking and expanding this particular energy center.

Engaging with your inner child, provided that the chakra exhibits activation, will initiate its restoration. Now is the opportune moment to raise the volume of the music, procure a remote control (and designate it as the microcosm of the musical composition), and commence an exuberant display of dancing, leaping, and vocalization.

Regarding the realm of lithotherapy, it is imperative to note the intricate equilibrium of the divine chakra. The vast majority of subconscious thoughts, comprising approximately 80%, ought to be approached with care in managing this particular energy center. Is there resonance between this chakra and all the orange stones? That is not always the case. The importance of color should not be overstated. Additionally, the stone possesses the energy required to provide "the".

We carefully selected the carnelian gemstone as our preferred choice for the sacred chakra's balance jewel (crafted with devotion in France), but our decision was not based solely on this factor. Smoked quartz possesses the capability to mitigate recurring patterns, allowing for the emergence of fresh perspectives.

The Esoteric Perception of the Chakras

The chakras originate from a philosophical framework derived from the religion of Hinduism. The initial recorded mention of this topic can be found in Sanskrit manuscripts. Individuals who subscribe to these convictions attribute them a tangible existence akin to other bodily organs, despite the fact that, in their composition, this physicality is considerably more nuanced. According to occult beliefs, it is claimed that clairvoyance perceives these objects as luminous and energetically charged focal points.

Scientists identified as 'independent researchers' undertaken the task of validating the presence of these points and providing rationale for their functionality. Numerous individuals, as reported by an estimated multitude, claim to possess the capacity to perceive and/or interact with these entities.

The individuals who evaluate the chakras classify them as vital organs. Their primary role would entail the meticulous oversight of the interplay of "energy" across diverse elements within the bodily system, as well as the harmonization of energy flow between the body, the terrestrial realm, and the celestial expanse. In light of the potential health risks faced by the person in question, they are exhibiting signs of stiffness or declining energy, congestion, or diminished vitality. They would engage in interpersonal communication and possess the capacity to mutually offset one another. On the other hand, a practice known as "energy harmonization" (such as acupuncture, even if it does not directly target the chakras) would have an impact on the individual's well-being.

Furthermore, it can be observed that the chakras align with the plexuses and glands, thereby indicating that their positions possess substantiated biological and psychological significance for the individual. However, in light of present understanding, physiology does not necessitate the utilization of the concept of chakra to elucidate the various observed phenomena.

According to esoteric beliefs, the manipūra-chakra is said to be situated at the solar plexus and consequently plays a significant part in the process of digestion. In regard to the sahasrâra-chakra, it resides at the anatomical level of the pineal gland, known for its production of melatonin, a hormone intricately linked to the regulation of sleep patterns. However, in the realm of occultism, it is imparted that the chakra, in its ethereal manifestation, serves as the conduit for regulating both the plexus and the corresponding gland, hence facilitating a gradual calibration and harmonization of the human psyche. In the event that sufficient secretion of the hormone originated from the pineal gland, a state of harmonious chakra would be achieved, thereby facilitating a restorative sleep for the individual. The scientist will contend that the refreshing sleep is attributable to the secretion of melatonin, whereas the occultist will assert that it is the activation of the sahasrâra-chakra that bestows this restful state (refer to scholarly resources such as the Wikipedia articles on Melatonin and Sleep).

In his book Kundalini-yoga, Sri Swami Shivananda delves deeper into the topic, asserting that the chakras, as detailed in an unspecified source, represent spiritual centers which can achieve their maximum activation through the ascent of Kundalini energy. Every chakra would serve as a receptacle for dormant, hidden sources of power. The melahadhara-chakra in a state of activation would grant the yogi the ability to achieve levitation and cleanse oneself from all moral transgressions. The activation of clairaudience would be facilitated by the vishuddha-chakra. The âjñâ-chakra would retain within him the latent potential for clairvoyant abilities. Once Sahasrâra is successfully activated, it would bestow upon us the ultimate tranquility, enabling us to attain a profound union with the cosmic entity.

WHAT DOES THE CONCEPT OF SPIRITUAL CONSCIOUSNESS ENTAIL?

The states of consciousness can be delineated as Higher and Lower consciousness, which exhibit contrasting characteristics. This denotes the transcendental nature of actuality. Divine awareness doesn't descend from above and effortlessly land in your possession. There are numerous challenges associated with achieving spiritual awareness, and it is inherently unfeasible to independently grasp this fundamental reality.

While we possess physical consciousness, our level of spiritual consciousness may not necessarily align. At the primary level of human experience, the mind becomes easily diverted and wanders with no clear direction or purpose. We perpetually pursue gratification through the acquisition of material goods, indulgence in physical intimacy, establishment of relationships, accumulation of wealth, and attainment of power, as the bounds to our satisfaction with worldly cravings appear boundless. The insatiable desire for constant acquisition is a result of an incomprehensible emptiness that individuals attempt to futilely satisfy through temporary worldly indulgences.

The void that permeates is precipitated by a dearth of cognizance regarding the eternal verity. In Hindu philosophy, the concept of absolute bliss is referred to as 'Sat Chit Anand', embodying the eternal and supreme principle of truth. An individual lacking the utmost knowledge is comparable to a vehicle with malfunctioning brakes, navigating through traffic at excessive velocity until encountering a collision or succumbing to unawareness, thereby becoming susceptible to despondency and self-indulgence. The human psyche can experience significant unease when aspirations remain unattained, resulting in a loss of tranquility and a sense of directionlessness.

An individual who desires to uncover the truth is encouraged to assume responsibility for the five senses, and to disengage the cognitive consciousness from its preoccupation with external stimuli. To exercise command over one's senses does not entail closing one's eyes or rendering one's ears deaf. The objective is to disengage one's consciousness from the perception of external objects, disassociating the mind from bodily awareness that encompasses the ego or any attachment to it, especially when it contradicts the absolute reality. The greatest deception that the human mind embraces is its attachment to worldly endeavors.

The essence of one's spiritual being is free from any misconceptions, and teachings in Eastern philosophy demonstrate that the cycle of birth and death serves the purpose of recognizing the ultimate reality and transcending lower levels of consciousness to achieve self-awareness. There exist two modalities of withdrawal, namely emotional withdrawal initially and subsequently philosophical withdrawal, from the inherent indulgences of worldly pursuits. Emotional withdrawal does not entail a detestation of worldly matters or a suppression of the desire to encounter them; rather, it signifies a transcendence of mundane existence when embarking upon the journey of self-realization and the pursuit of ultimate truth.

Those individuals who have not yet experienced the transcendental bliss of the ultimate truth often harbor concerns that engaging in spiritual practices necessitates renouncing the material world, retreating to secluded mountainous regions, and enduring austere living conditions. This is not true. An individual possessing spiritual consciousness can effectively reside within society while actively participating in worldly activities; in other words, they become impervious to the misleading perceptions that once impacted them. He embraces life to its utmost and derives greater contentment than those who pursue materialistic indulgences.

The Five Bodies

According to the teachings of Eastern esoteric yoga, it is believed that individuals possess not only a physical body, but also a set of interconnected multidimensional bodies known as "Khoshas" or etheric layers. Envision an onion and conceptualize each khosha as a stratum that encapsulates the 'Self,' also referred to as the Atman or The Ultimate Truth. In pursuit of the ultimate verity, individuals of spiritual and religious inclination employ diverse techniques in their quest for self-discovery.

Physical – Annamaya kosha: The term "Anna" pertains to sustenance. All material aspects of existence are transient, inevitably succumbing to the engulfing forces of peripheral reality. Therefore, the outermost layer of the khoshas is referred to as the food sheath, or Annamaya khosha.

In the practice of Vedanta, individuals diligently cultivate and nourish this facet of their being, ensuring that it serves as a conduit for external experiences while maintaining internal focus, unobstructed by any impediments during the practice of meditation. This physical entity possesses the most minimal oscillations and is interconnected with the ethereal and celestial realms.

Energy - Pranamaya kosha: Prana signifies the intrinsic life force, responsible for generating intricate vibrations associated with respiration. These potent forces underpin the physical elements of sensory perception and physiological functioning within the corporal entity. According to Vedanta, it is beneficial and imperative for individuals pursuing a wholesome existence and engaging in meditation to ensure appropriate training, regulation, and guidance to ensure the seamless flow of this aspect of their being. The energetic or ethereal body possesses a frequency of oscillation that is superior to that of the corporeal body, although inferior to the celestial body.

Mental - The Manamaya kosha pertains to the aspect of the mind responsible for the processing of thoughts and emotions. It exercises direct authority over bodily functions by means of prana, assuming the role of a supervisor by providing instructions. When provided with explicit instructions from the higher echelons, it operates efficiently. Nevertheless, when it becomes clouded by its illusions, the profound wisdom becomes obscured.

After attending to the well-being of the physical body and cultivating the energy of prana, the paramount aspect that necessitates positive cultivation is the realm of consciousness at hand. During the process of meditation, individuals can develop an awareness of the Manamaya khosha, thoroughly investigate it, and subsequently delve deeper into the inner realms encompassing the other koshas. This entity also transcends temporal and spatial boundaries. Sophisticated practitioners of remote viewing engage in telepathic communication through the utilization of their cognitive faculties.

Wisdom - The cognitive facet referred to as the Gyanmaya kosha pertains to the acquisition and application of knowledge, representing a deeper layer of understanding that lies beneath the analytical and contemplative aspects of the intellect. It exhibits awareness and possesses the ability to discern between what is morally correct and incorrect. It represents the degree of ego awareness, which encompasses the potent surge of self-identifying consciousness. The inherent state of "I Am-ness" exerts a constructive impact, but when it becomes intertwined with recollections and becomes obscured by the faculties of the mind and body, it diminishes its affirmative potency.

A fundamental element of spiritual practice involves the acquisition of heightened awareness at this particular plane of our existence. The pursuit of Truth at its utmost elevation is to delve into the depths of one's being, in quest of the eternal core of consciousness. Furthermore, this entity possesses the ability to retain previous life experiences in the form of holographic images.

Bliss – Anandamaya kosha: Ananda denotes the state of profound joy, representing the deepest layer among the koshas, positioned as the foremost layer encompassing the Atman (Soul), the eternal essence of consciousness. Nevertheless, it is not a state of bliss limited to the realm of the mind's periphery. Ananda exists as an entirely distinct realm of existence, separate from the realm of consciousness.

Beneath and transcending the realm of cognition, lies an enduring state of tranquility, bliss, and unswerving affection that remains impervious to rationality or external stimuli, evading any propensity for joyful psychological responses. It manifests as mere existence, tranquil in its inherent state of euphoria. (It is alternatively referred to as "Sat-Chit-Anand.")

Atman – Self: The epitome of enlightenment is referred to as the Self, the timeless center of awareness, as it is devoid of birth and mortality. Atman has been elucidated as "the ineffable" and is referred to as "the formless and attributeless" in Vedanta. All forms of spiritual and religious endeavors guide us on a journey towards introspection, delving deep into our innermost essence.

Three- Equilibrium Compared to a Lack of Equilibrium

When there is a harmonious equilibrium within your chakras, a sense of tranquility will be experienced. One should not experience any form of physical discomfort such as pain, tightness, or stiffness in their body, nor encounter any manner of negative emotions such as nervousness, fear, or doubt. These indicators indicate that you are experiencing a lack of equilibrium. Any form of unease, whether it pertains to physical, psychological, or emotional well-being, is indicative of an underlying disharmony within your chakras. When there is equilibrium in the chakras, an individual will experience a comprehensive state of physical and mental harmony.

There exist numerous methods for discerning a disturbance in the alignment of one's chakras. Every chakra will manifest distinct physical and emotional symptoms as a means to communicate any underlying issues to the individual. If an individual exerts diligent and unwavering scrutiny upon their physical, mental, and emotional facets, they ought to promptly identify any disparities and undertake the requisite measures to rectify them.

When the fundamental chakra achieves equilibrium, an individual will experience a sense of security and stability. Nevertheless, in the event of an inequity, the individual may experience apprehension regarding their ability to adequately sustain themselves or fulfill their fundamental requirements for survival. It is important to bear in mind that each chakra will manifest physical symptoms, and given that the base chakra is situated at the lower end of the spinal column, it may manifest various physical symptoms such as afflictions in the lower extremities, anus, coccyx, male reproductive organs, prostate gland, and the immune system. In the event that any of these physical ailments manifest, failure to address them promptly may potentially give rise to subsequent complications. A few additional matters that may be encompassed are sciatica, knee discomfort, constipation, degenerative arthritis, and a condition related to dietary habits.

As previously discussed, the sacral chakra is situated in the lower abdominal region and serves as a focal point for channeling and comprehending one's interpersonal connections with fellow individuals. This energy is also interconnected with the entirety of external power. These encompass various facets, including addictive behaviors, fixations, dominance, sexualized pursuits, and monetary preoccupations, all of which may exert a significant influence over an individual. This chakra additionally facilitates the capacity to embrace others, as well as novel encounters. When the equilibrium of this chakra is attained, an individual will experience a profound sense of interconnectedness, unconditional love, and unwavering emotional security within their interpersonal connections. Nevertheless, in the event of an inequity, an individual may experience a hindrance in wholeheartedly dedicating themselves to a relationship, a difficulty in effectively communicating their feelings, and a general incapability of unwinding or lowering their defenses. They might experience profound emotions of betrayal and helplessness. Certain physiological afflictions that may become apparent include urinary impairments, renal complications, discomfort in the hips, pelvis, and lower back, alongside sexual and reproductive dysfunctions.

It is understood that the solar plexus chakra is situated within the upper abdominal region. It serves as the hub of vitality, intimately connected to an individual's assurance, value, pride, and inherent strength. It is the vitality that empowers an individual to experience self-assurance and exert influence over their existence.

When equilibrium is achieved in this energy, an individual will experience feelings of self-compassion and self-esteem. They will experience a sense of assurance, self-assurance, and mastery. Nevertheless, in the presence of an inequity, an individual might experience a deterioration in their self-worth and exhibit a severe lack of self-assurance. They might experience profound anxieties related to the possibility of being rejected, concerns about their physical appearance, as well as fear of being criticized. Certain physical maladies that could potentially arise include persistent fatigue, elevated blood pressure, gastric ulcers, diabetes mellitus, gastrointestinal disorders, hepatic impairment, conditions affecting the colon, as well as pancreatic and gallbladder complications.

The heart chakra, as you may be aware, is positioned within the thoracic region, situated slightly above the cardiac muscle. This energy governs all matters pertaining to affection and connections, pardon and benevolence. When this chakra achieves a state of equilibrium, an individual shall experience sensations of thankfulness and elation. Trust can be acquired, and an individual with a harmoniously functioning heart chakra will readily manifest forgiveness and compassion. When the equilibrium of this chakra is disrupted, an individual may experience emotions such as envy, neglect, resentment, and fury. At times, they may exhibit an excessive degree of affection, leading to a sense of emotional confinement within themselves. In instances of heart chakra imbalance, individuals may experience an all-encompassing sensation of solitude, irrespective of their activities or the company they keep. A selection of the physical ailments that may arise as a consequence of an imbalance in the heart chakra encompass heart disease, pulmonary ailments, asthma, issues pertaining to the upper back and shoulders, discomfort in the arms and wrists, as well as complications involving the breasts and the lymphatic system.

The throat chakra governs our capacity to adeptly articulate our thoughts, emotions, desires, and necessities, and it naturally resides within the throat region. When equilibrium is achieved in this particular chakra, an individual gains the freedom to fully articulate themselves. They exhibit a strong commitment to truthfulness and integrity, all while maintaining assertiveness in articulating their desires and needs, and establishing suitable limits. In the event of an imbalance in the throat chakra, an individual may encounter difficulties in effectively articulating oneself, often attributable to apprehension or anxiety. They might perceive a lack of agency in respect to all matters. Typically, they possess a limited degree of determination and perceive themselves as having no agency in the events surrounding them. It is probable that they will encounter difficulties in various modes of communication, encompassing both oral and nonverbal aspects. A potential consequence of an imbalance in this particular chakra are certain physical manifestations.

The third eye chakra can be found positioned on the brow, situated between the eyes. This particular chakra enables an individual to perceive, comprehend, and appraise the broader aspects and interconnectedness of a situation. Furthermore, it grants them the ability to gain insights into both their internal psyche and the external environment. When the third eye chakra is in a state of equilibrium, an individual will experience a heightened sense of concentration, mental clarity, and an ability to discern reality from illusion without difficulty. Individuals with a properly aligned and harmonious eye chakra will possess a receptive disposition towards gaining perspective and sagacity from their fellow beings. Nonetheless, in the event of an imbalance within the eye chakra, individuals may frequently engage in daydreaming and exhibit a propensity for possessing an overly embellished imagination. They may exhibit a propensity for persistent emotional instability, coupled with an inability to effectively assimilate knowledge from external sources or acknowledge, confront, and overcome their own apprehensions. Certain physical ailments that may frequently arise due to an imbalance in these chakras include sinus ailments, headaches, impaired vision, eye strain, auditory impairment, disrupted hormone regulation, and, in severe instances, seizures.

www.ingramcontent.com/pod-product-compliance
Lightning Source LLC
Chambersburg PA
CBHW050401120526
44590CB00015B/1776